HOW
TO BE A
GENTLEMAN

How
TO BE A
Gentleman

A
CONTEMPORARY
GUIDE TO
COMMON
COURTESY

JOHN BRIDGES

RUTLEDGE HILL PRESS®

Nashville, Tennessee

A Thomas Nelson Company

Illustrations by Alicia Adkerson, Adkerson Design

Published by Rutledge Hill Press, a Thomas Nelson Company, P.O. Box 141000, Nashville, Tennessee 37214.

Typography by E. T. Lowe Typesetting, Inc.

Design by Bateman Design

Library of Congress Cataloging-in-Publication Data

Bridges, John. 1950–
    How to be a gentleman : an uncommon guide to
contemporary courtesy / John Bridges.
        p.   cm.
    ISBN 1-55853-596-9
    1. Etiquette for men. I. Title.
BJ1601.B76 1998
395.1'42—dc21

                                                    98-10379
                                                    CIP

Printed in the United States of America

        7 8 9—02 01

For
CLAY ISAACS,
who was born knowing
all these things

CONTENTS

INTRODUCTION

For decades—maybe centuries—men have depended on women to set the rules for polite behavior. Sometimes that woman was the man's mother; sometimes she was his wife; sometimes she was a famous etiquette expert like Amy Vanderbilt or Emily Post.

There comes a time in every man's life when his mother isn't around any more. Married or not, he is expected to go to parties and to entertain. He has business associates to deal with and coworkers with whom he must get along. Such moments can fill a guy with needless terror. He may get frustrated trying to tie a bow tie or set his table correctly. He may find himself fumbling when he needs to introduce two of his best friends.

The truth of the matter is, being a gentleman is not rocket science. Being a gentleman requires a little logic, a bit of forethought, and a great deal of consideration for others. It is not about complicated rules and convoluted instructions. Instead, it is about trying to make life easier for other people. It is about honestly and sincerely being a nice guy.

For a guy the noblest virtues are camaraderie, dependability, and unswerving loyalty. It confuses him to think that his future might be ruined if he ate his entrée with a salad fork.

That is why this book spells out what a man really needs to know if he plans to make his way in this world.

Simply acting like a gentleman is not enough. It is being a gentleman that is important, and that means thinking of others, being there when you are needed, and knowing when you are not needed. It is what you do and who you are—an accumulation of gentlemanly behaviors over the course of a lifetime—that make a man a gentleman.

It truly is possible for a man to learn to be a gentleman if he has the direction he needs. For that reason, the women of the world will be glad this book exists.

Chapter One

A GENTLEMAN EXPERIENCES REAL LIFE

A gentleman knows how to make
others feel comfortable.

———

A gentleman knows how to make
a grilled cheese at 2 A.M. and
an omelet at 7 A.M.

———

If a gentleman has a cold, especially if
he is running a fever, he declines all
social invitations. If it is possible,
he even stays away from the office.

———

Even if he lives alone, a gentleman
never drinks milk directly from
the container.

———

A GENTLEMAN ATTENDS THE THEATER

Because he respects other people, a gentleman always shows up on time for any performance, whether it is a concert, a motion picture, or a stage play. If he arrives late, he does not attempt to be seated until there is a suitable break in the performance. (In the case of a play or a musical comedy, his tardiness may require him to wait until intermission.) In every case, he follows the instructions of the ushers. If he behaves himself, a gentleman knows, a kindly usher may quietly slip him into a seat on the back row.

A gentleman never forgets that watching a live performance is not the same thing as watching a TV show in his own living room. He does not talk during the performance—even during the very loudest music or sound effects. He does not shift about in his seat unnecessarily. And, if he has a tendency to cough, he always carries a cough drop. Should a gentleman find himself surprised by an uncontrollable coughing jag, he leaves the auditorium—both for his own good and for the good of others.

At a concert or any other musical performance, a gentleman does not applaud until the end of a complete musical number. If he is unsure he would be well-advised not to start an ovation alone.

———

If a gentleman is lost, he admits it. He readily asks for directions.

———

A gentleman does not pick his nose in public. In fact, he is wise if he does not pick his nose in private, since bad habits are far too easily formed.

————

When a gentleman walks his dog, he assumes responsibility for his pet's poop.

————

When a gentleman arrives late for a church service, he waits for a suitable pause in the service before slipping, as unobtrusively as possible, into a pew at the back.

————

In a theater, a church, or any place where people have gathered to hear music, a gentleman always turns his beeper off.

————

A GENTLEMAN ATTENDS
A WEDDING

Obviously, a gentleman only attends weddings to which he has been invited. If his invitation does not say "and guest," he attends alone, even if a reception follows. He arrives on time and sits on the appropriate side of the aisle (the left side, if he is a friend of the bride; the right side, if he is a friend of the groom; if he knows them both, he sits on the side with the greater number of empty seats). During the ceremony, he stands when everyone else does, and he does not chat during the music. At the reception he speaks to the bride and groom and to their parents (no matter how many divorces are involved). If there is dancing, he does his part, partnering as many bridesmaids as possible.

A gentleman does not carry a cellular phone into a theater.

———

If a gentleman has left a message for another person, he does not leave badgering follow-up calls, especially if no deadline is involved. A gentleman is not obliged to return unsolicited messages or voice mail.

———

A gentleman who happens to be a doctor checks his beeper with an usher or changes it to the silent setting. However, if he is a real estate agent out for an evening at the theater, he leaves his beeper or cellular phone at home. A real-estate closing is not a life-threatening emergency.

———

A gentleman does not hesitate to screen his calls.

———

In the workout room, a gentleman does not hog the weights.

———

If a gentleman tends to have athlete's foot, he wears shower shoes at the gym.

———

A gentleman may do what he pleases in his own shower, but he does not shave in the shower at the gym. He never takes another gentleman's towel.

———

If a gentleman shaves at the health club, he always rinses out the sink.

———

A gentleman knows that the gym is a place for working out, not merely a place for socializing, and certainly not a place for showing off.

———

A GENTLEMAN ATTENDS
A FUNERAL

A gentleman recognizes that a funeral is a time for paying respects. He wears a dark suit, a white shirt, a somber tie, and a pair of black shoes. If there is a wake, a reception, or a visitation with the deceased family, he arrives on time and waits quietly in the receiving line. He keeps his remarks simple out of respect for the grieving person's overwrought emotions. A statement such as, "I am sorry about your loss, Mrs. Jones. Your husband was a wonderful person," is appropriate. During the service, a gentleman does not engage the other mourners in conversation. He sits where the ushers tell him to sit. He always signs the book.

A gentleman may attend the funeral of anyone he has known personally or professionally, at least if they have been on speaking terms. If the deceased person has shown him particular kindness—especially if he has ever been entertained in the deceased person's home—a gentleman makes a point to show his respects.

For reasons of courtesy *and* safety, a gentleman does not dawdle at the automated teller machine. If other people are in line behind him, he does not waste time, checking all his savings account balances. He completes his transaction and moves on.

———

A gentleman never eats his lunch while he is behind the wheel of a vehicle.

———

A gentleman knows how to behave in other people's churches. If the congregation stands, he stands. He does not, however, have to cross himself, bow, or kneel.

———

If a gentleman attends synagogue and is offered a yarmulke (the traditional headcovering worn by men at Conservative and Orthodox Jewish services), he puts it on.

———

If a gentleman attends a great many bar mitzvahs and bat mitzvahs, he buys his own yarmulke.

———

A gentleman does not assume it is the other person's responsibility to provide the condoms.

———

A GENTLEMAN WALKS THROUGH A DOOR

A gentleman always glances behind him when he walks through a door. He never slams a door in another person's face. It does not matter whether the other person is a man or a woman.

If it is a revolving door, a gentleman pays more attention than usual. He steps ahead, does not move too fast, pushes the door open, and makes the world a little easier for the person after him. That is, after all, why gentlemen exist. He never shares a revolving door section with another person. He respects their space. Besides, in big cities, that's where pickpockets do their business.

A gentleman does not put his groceries on the conveyor belt with another shopper's purchases.

———

If a gentleman eats in bed, he always changes the sheets.

———

When a gentleman is finished with the dryer, he cleans the lint filter.

———

At the Laundromat, a gentleman never takes another person's laundry out of the washer or the dryer, no matter how long he has been waiting. If he is in a hurry, he asks for the attendant's assistance. If there is no attendant, he chooses another Laundromat.

———

A GENTLEMAN GOES THROUGH A CHECKOUT LINE

A gentleman always keeps an accurate count of the items in his grocery cart. He does not try to slip through the express checkout line if he has exceeded the posted limit. On the other hand, if he has only a couple of items, and a kind person invites him to step ahead in line, he graciously accepts the offer. He is not bashful about asking for the type of bag he wants, but otherwise he does not make any serious demands on the cashier. When it is time to pay the total, a gentleman has his checkbook, cash, or credit card ready. A gentleman does not cause a delay in the checkout line. He realizes that there are people with spoiling milk in their baskets and hungry children at home. As a gentleman, he knows it is his job to make the checkout lines of life move along.

If a gentleman must inconvenience other people by stepping over their feet in a theater—or when leaving his seat on an airplane—he offers an occasional "Excuse me." If he must leave the theater in the middle of the performance, he does not say anything and does his best not to step on toes.

———

A gentleman does not use his car horn indiscriminately. On the other hand, he is not sheepish about giving an occasional honk to avert disaster.

———

A gentleman uses his turn signals.

———

A gentleman parks his car carefully. He does not bang his car door into the car next to him. If he scratches another car, he leaves a note.

———

THE ETIQUETTE
OF THE CIGAR

A gentleman savors a cigar in the same way that he savors a good glass of whiskey—only on occasion and never to excess. He knows it is an acquired taste, and that to some nonsmokers its fumes may be even more repellent than cigarette smoke.

Before smoking, a gentleman makes sure cigars are permitted. Once his cigar is lit, he does not puff so that noxious clouds of smoke surround his face, and he does not allow his cigar to accumulate a long, fragile column of ash that might shatter, spoiling his shirt front or the table linens.

When a gentleman's cigar is finished, he puts it in an ashtray. When he is in a public place and in the company of others, he resists all temptation to chew on a sodden stump of stogie.

A GENTLEMAN TAKES AN AIRPLANE FLIGHT

Almost invariably, the passengers on an airplane have been brought together by a mix of chance and necessity. A gentleman understands that, in such situations, it is important for everyone to abide by the rules.

He brings on board only the amount of luggage that is permitted. He is careful when he stows it overhead to prevent injury to his fellow passengers and to himself. If a bag or parcel is small enough, he stows it under the seat in front of him. He does not intrude on space that is allotted for another passenger's use. He sits in the seat that is assigned to him. If he has sat in the wrong seat, and if he is asked to move, he does not argue about it. He gets up and finds the place to which he has been assigned. On the other hand, he feels no obligation to give up his rightful seat to another person.

If it is at all possible, a gentleman stays in his seat throughout the entire flight. A trip to the bathroom is almost the only excuse to do otherwise. On long flights a gentleman with a health condition does not hesitate to leave his seat for a short time to stretch out his legs and get his blood circulating. When he must leave his seat, a gentleman excuses himself as unobtrusively as possible, making sure not to step on other passengers' feet.

An airplane flight is one of the few instances in life when it is entirely appropriate for two people to be together for several hours and never speak at all. They may begin the flight as strangers and end it the same way, without anyone having reason to feel neglected or abused.

If the hour is terribly early or extremely late, a gentleman does not phone a private residence.

———

A gentleman turns the television down after ten o'clock. If he must listen to music at three o'clock in the morning, he buys himself a good pair of headphones.

———

At sporting events, a gentleman feels free to stand up and shout during exciting moments. Otherwise, he keeps his seat. He does not begrudge the other team its victory. If his own team is the victor, he does not taunt the opposition.

———

A gentleman does not take his pets to other people's houses, unless he is specifically urged to do so.

———

A gentleman does not feel obliged to invite other people's pets to his house.

———

If a gentleman is around another person's dog, he does not tease that dog or encourage it to bark.

———

A gentleman does not touch other people's children, unless he is invited to do so. Neither does he overexcite them.

———

To establish a friendly relationship with the hotel concierge, a gentleman asks the concierge for some necessary service, one that is important enough to justify a substantial tip.

———

If a bellhop offers to assist a gentleman in hailing a cab, a gentleman accepts the offer, understanding that a tip is implied.

———

A gentleman never feels that he must say pleasant things about unpleasant people. Even when describing pleasant people, he does not stretch the truth. Goodness, when accurately described, can stand on its own.

––––

If a gentleman must leave the dinner table, he simply says, "Excuse me." It does not matter whether he is headed for the telephone booth or the bathroom. No further explanation is necessary.

––––

If a gentleman borrows another person's property—whether it is a power drill, a new bestseller, or a set of salad forks— he sets a deadline by which he plans to return it. He keeps to that deadline and returns the property in good condition.

––––

A gentleman does not adjust
his crotch in public.

––––––

A gentleman knows that it is a very
dangerous thing to ask another person,
"What do you want for Christmas?" At
best, the answer will be, "I don't know—
surprise me." At worst, it will be
something a gentleman cannot provide.
In either case, the answer will be
something a gentleman does not want
to hear. He will be better off if he
watches and listens closely.

––––––

A gentleman never makes a date out of
desperation.

––––––

If a gentleman must chew tobacco, he
chews it outdoors. He does not keep a
drool cup on his desk.

––––––

When a gentleman recognizes friends and acquaintances at other tables in a restaurant, he feels free to greet them, but only in the least intrusive way possible. He may stop by their table to greet them cordially, but he does not interrupt their dinner or their conversation for long.

—————

A gentleman always offers to share his umbrella.

—————

When a gentleman makes his way down a row in a crowded theater, he faces the people who are already in their seats. A gentleman never forces others to stare at his backside.

—————

Chapter Two

A GENTLEMAN GETS DRESSED

In warm weather a gentleman always wears an undershirt.

———

Unless he is a Texas Ranger or a cattle rancher, a gentleman does not wear cowboy boots with a suit.

———

When a gentleman wears a double-breasted suit, he never leaves the jacket unbuttoned.

———

A gentleman's pants cuffs fall in a gentle break over his shoes. When he stands, his socks do not show.

———

A gentleman clips his nose hairs and the unsightly hair in his ears. As he grows older, he may need to trim his eyebrows.

———

A gentleman tucks his undershirt into his undershorts.

———

A gentleman does not carry unnecessary paraphernalia in his pockets. A bulky key ring or a Swiss army knife destroys the line of even the most expensive pair of slacks.

———

A gentleman has his shoes shined.

———

A GENTLEMAN AND HIS COLOGNE

A gentleman considers cologne intimate apparel. It should not cause comment, positive or negative, among other people in the room. Instead, it should be saved as a pleasant surprise for people with whom he makes close physical contact. A gentleman understands that cologne is, after all, an accessory. It is not to be used as a substitute for deodorant. A dab on either side of the neck, with another drop on a gentleman's pocket handkerchief, is quite enough.

When used to excess, cologne is annoying and raises questions about what smells are being covered up. Anytime a person can identify the brand of scent that a man is wearing, he is wearing too much.

When the weather is cold, a gentleman always wears gloves, and not just to keep his hands warm. He knows that cold fingers do not make for a pleasant handshake.

———

If there is no polish involved, a gentleman occasionally has a manicure.

———

A gentleman always lets his suit jacket or sports coat air out overnight before he returns it to the closet.

———

A gentleman feels no necessity to wear socks after Memorial Day—at least in casual situations. If he is southern, he may not even wear them to church.

———

WHEN TO WEAR
BROWN SHOES

A gentleman knows that even today, black shoes are considered more formal, businesslike, and serious than brown shoes. In fact, in certain businesses—the legal profession, for instance, or banking—black shoes remain the only truly acceptable footwear.

On the other hand, if a gentleman is in a situation where a brown or green suit or a sports coat would be acceptable—in an office with a more relaxed dress code or at a dressy sporting event, for example—his brown shoes will serve him well.

However, a gentleman never wears brown shoes to a funeral or to a wedding. If he is fortunate enough to have a long life, he will live through many weekends, and his brown loafers will get plenty of wear.

A GENTLEMAN AND HIS CAP

A gentleman will probably own a stack of baseball caps, which he wears after work, on weekends, or on casual days at the office. He may feel that a beloved baseball cap is almost a part of his body, but he should never forget that it is still a *hat* and that common courtesy demands it be treated as such.

A gentleman does not wear his cap inside most public buildings—especially houses of worship. Traditionally, a gentleman would remove his hat if he were greeting a woman or being introduced to a new acquaintance of either sex. If a man wears a cap to cover up an unwashed mass of hair or to disguise a balding head, he need not remove it. He gives tug to his cap brim out of respect for the other person— and as a wistful acknowledgment of courtesy long past.

A gentleman washes his hair
regularly, and he makes every effort to
prevent dandruff.

———

When a gentleman feels the urge
to color his mustache, he shaves
his mustache off.

———

If a gentleman is given to wearing
outlandish hats—such as a deerstalker
or a Russian sable cap with earflaps—
he understands that he will probably
attract attention.

———

A gentleman never wears a belt when he
is wearing suspenders.

———

When a gentleman wears his black tie with a wing collar, he always positions the points of the collar *behind* the tie. That way, the ends of the tie can help hold the stiffened collar down.

————

A gentleman ties his own tie. Especially if it is a bow tie. Especially if it is black.

————

A gentleman's shirt studs need not match his cuff links precisely. However, they always complement each another.

————

When a gentleman wears a cummerbund, he makes sure the pleats are turned up. (In that way, they can actually be used as tiny, secret pockets, perhaps for the safekeeping of theater tickets.)

————

WHEN TO WEAR A TUXEDO

A gentleman never wears a tuxedo before six o'clock, no matter what anyone else does. If he owns his dinner clothes— the correct term for what is known as a tuxedo—he wears them anytime the invitation says "black tie" or "black tie optional." Likewise, if he is attending any formal event—a wedding reception or a dance—that begins after eight in the evening, he may assume that black tie is appropriate.

However, if he knows that other guests at the party are unlikely to be dressed in dinner clothes, he plays it safe and wears a dark suit. If the invitation does not indicate any dress code, or if "black tie optional" is suggested, a gentleman does not feel obligated to rent dinner clothes. In such situations, his dark suit will serve him perfectly well.

How to tie a bow tie

Tying a bow tie is, essentially, like tying any other bow. A gentleman knows this, and he does not become frustrated if he fumbles the first few times he attempts the procedure. Instead, he gives himself enough practice at home when he does not have a pressing dinner date.

1. Adjust the length of the tie. (A shorter tie will result in a smaller bow. If the tie is left long, the end product has a fluffier, less-tailored look.)

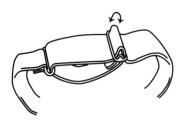

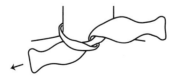

2. Put the tie around your neck. Leave one end hanging longer than the other.

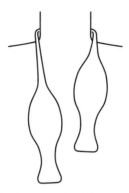

3. Bring the long end of the tie over the short end. Then pull it up from behind, just as if you were beginning a granny knot.

4. Tug securely on both ends.

5. Fold the short end of the tie over to
   make a loop.

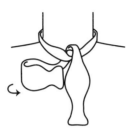

6. Bring the long end of the tie up, over,
   and around the middle of the entire
   package.

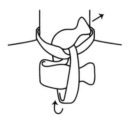

7. Fold the remaining part of the long end
   into a loop and stuff it through the
   opening behind the short end. (The
   loop of the long end must end up
   behind the flat part of the short end.)

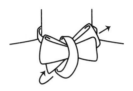

8. Tug on the tie and twist it about until it
   takes on a neatly finished look. (This
   step may take some time, but do not
   give up. It really will work. Just
   remember to tug on both loops at the
   same time, just as if you were
   tightening your shoelaces. Otherwise,
   the bow will come undone.)

A gentleman never colors his hair.

———

Although a gentleman usually takes his shirts to a laundry, he also knows how to use an iron and a can of spray starch.

———

A gentleman owns at least one pair of black lace-up shoes.

———

Even if a gentleman has to rent his dinner clothes, he wears something that is not borrowed. A good pair of links is enough.

———

When a gentleman wears a vest, he leaves the bottom button undone.

———

When a gentleman outgrows his clothes, he gives them away to charity. He does not pretend that someday he will lose weight. When, and if, he does lose weight, he certainly will not want to celebrate by wearing out-of-date clothes.

———

A gentleman never wears a button-down collar with a bow tie.

———

When necessary, a gentleman has his shoes resoled.

———

A gentleman never wears the same pair
of blue jeans two days in a row.

———

A gentleman's pants are always
cuffed except for his blue jeans
and his formal trousers.

———

A gentleman never has creases ironed
into the legs of his jeans.

———

Chapter Three

A GENTLEMAN GOES
TO DINNER

A gentleman knows when it is all right
to eat the garnish.

————

When a gentleman has an unpleasant
time in a restaurant, he does not badger
the wait staff. He lodges his complaint
with the management. Unless he is a
glutton for punishment, he does not go
back to that restaurant.

————

After business hours, a gentleman
does not carry his cellular phone
into a restaurant.

————

How to Leave a Tip

Tipping is a delicate matter that concerns only the gentleman and the server. He does not brag about leaving a generous gratuity. If the service has been inferior, a gentleman does not inform his companions that he plans to leave a less-than-sizable tip.

A gentleman should leave a tip in a restaurant or a bar but not at a fast-food establishment. To recognize good service, he leaves at least 15 percent of his total bill. Excellent, attentive service justifies a tip of 20 percent or more. If the service has been minimally acceptable, however, a gentleman may leave only 10 percent. If he is so dissatisfied that he feels the urge to leave less, he leaves nothing and explains his actions to the manager. Angrily leaving a dime or a quarter demonstrates that the customer and the server are equally ill mannered.

If the food set before him is intended
to be eaten piping-hot (or icy cold),
and if a gentleman is the first person
to be served at his table, he waits
for one other person to be served,
and then he begins to eat.

––––––

If a gentleman's meal is slow to arrive
from the kitchen, and if others at the
table have been served, he urges them,
"Please, go ahead without me."
And he means it.

––––––

If a gentleman is on a diet, he does not
talk about it at the table.

––––––

If a gentleman has not made a dinner
reservation, he accepts the fact that he
will have to wait in the bar.

––––––

A gentleman does not talk with his mouth full.

––––––

A gentleman knows to start with the fork on the outside. If the salad fork is in the wrong place, he does not make a scene.

––––––

When a gentleman has finished eating, he places his knife and his fork, criss-crossed, on his plate. He never places a piece of dirty flatware back on the table.

––––––

Once a gentleman's dinner knife has been dirtied, he never lets it touch the tablecloth.

––––––

A gentleman never salts his food before tasting it. He would never insult the cook in that way.

––––––

How to know
which fork to use

If the table has been set correctly, a
gentleman has no problem knowing which
fork, spoon, or knife to pick up first. When
he sits down at the table, he will find his
flatware and his cutlery set out in the order
in which he will need it. When the first
course arrives, he uses the fork that is the
farthest away from his plate. When he is
finished with that course, he leaves his
fork on his plate, and it is taken away. He
proceeds in the same manner throughout
the meal so that by the time dessert rolls
around, he will have only one fork, spoon,
or knife left. If, by chance the flatware has
been arranged in the wrong order, a
gentleman still follows this logical system.
In such cases, the person setting the table
has caused the confusion.

A GENTLEMAN AND
HIS VEGETARIAN FRIENDS

Even if a gentleman is an inveterate steak eater, he is likely to find himself playing host to people who choose not to eat meat. (Sometimes, they will scorn all meat, even all dairy products. They may limit themselves to white meats, such as fish and chicken.) When a gentleman entertains guests who are vegetarians, he attempts to honor their wishes and make sure they enjoy an appetizing, satisfying meal. When selecting a restaurant, he checks that the menu includes a variety of salads and pasta dishes. If he is selecting a menu ahead of time, he arranges to have available a vegetarian option.

If a gentleman himself is a vegetarian, he does not ask to be coddled. If his decision not to eat meat is a matter of deep conviction, he informs his host or hostess about it, ahead of time, so that the proper arrangements can be made. When he accepts an invitation, he may say, "Of course, I'd love to come for dinner on Saturday. I'm a vegetarian, you know, but otherwise, I'll eat anything that's set before me." For better or worse, the vegetarian usually is the exception to the rule. It is his responsibility to let his host or hostess know about his special needs.

When faced with a plate of long pasta—such as spaghetti, linguine, or fettucine—a gentleman resists every temptation to chop it up with his knife and fork. Instead, he twirls a manageable mouthful around the tines of his fork and, with the help of his spoon, transfers it to his mouth.

How to make
A DINNER RESERVATION

A gentleman realizes that a dinner
reservation is a verbal contract between
him and the restaurant. He does not make
reservations unless he actually plans to use
them, and if he must cancel or if the size
of his party changes, he informs the
restaurant as far ahead of time as possible.

A gentleman does not take it as a
personal affront if a restaurant is unable to
seat his party at the time he requests. If he
is unable to accept a reservation at an
earlier or later hour, a gentleman asks for a
recommendation of another establishment.

If his party has special requirements—
seating in a smoking or nonsmoking area,
for example—he makes those requests
when he reserves the table.

If a hostess, a manager, or a maître d' has
been particularly helpful in arranging a

gentleman's reservation, he gladly acknowledges that service with a tip. However, he presents that tip as unostentatiously as possible, perhaps slipping it into the hostess's palm in the midst of a parting handshake.

A gentleman knows that people who do not claim their reservations will quickly gain a reputation for being rude and inconsiderate.

In a restaurant a gentleman observes the established dress code. If he is not sure if a jacket is required, he asks ahead of time. If he has invited other gentlemen to dinner, he lets them know if a jacket is necessary or not.

HOW TO ORDER
A BOTTLE OF WINE

A gentleman orders a wine he likes or a wine one of his dinner companions suggests. That does not mean that he must order the most expensive wine on the list. When a suggested wine is out of his price range, he orders something else, with no apologies to anyone.

In general, red wine is still the wine of choice to accompany red meat, pasta dishes with tomato sauces, and most heavy entrées. White wines are usually selected to accompany fish, chicken, salads, and pasta dishes with light sauces. However, a gentleman may feel at ease ordering any wine he likes.

When a gentleman has ordered a bottle of wine, it will be presented to him by the server, who will show him the label (so that a gentleman can see that he is, in truth, being served what he ordered) and then offer him the cork (so that a gentleman can see that it is not too dry). The server will then pour a sip of wine in the gentleman's glass. The gentleman performs a quick taste test, and if the wine passes muster, he allows the server to pour it, first for the gentleman's guests and then for the gentleman himself.

The server may leave the wine, if it is white, in a cooler at tableside. If it is red, he may leave it on the table. In either case, a gentleman may wait for the server to return to refill empty glasses, or he may take care of that duty himself.

When a gentleman chooses not to drink wine, he feels perfectly confident in telling the waiter, "No thank you. I'll just have some water [or some iced tea or some soda]."

When a gentleman pours a glass of wine, he finishes by turning the bottle slightly, which prevents unsightly dribbles and drips.

———

A gentleman never crunches on his ice cubes except in the privacy of his home.

———

A gentleman does not attempt to change the opinions of his dinner companions. A seated dinner is not a debate tournament.

———

A gentleman never drinks a cocktail through a straw.

———

At the dinner table, a gentleman helps the woman to the right of him as she sits or rises from her chair.

———

How to use
a dinner napkin

After a gentleman takes his seat at a dinner table, his first action is always to place his dinner napkin in his lap. He *always* places it in his lap. He does not tuck it into his belt or under his chin. A gentleman does not wait for a server to handle his napkin for him. (Only in the most ostentatious restaurants do servers treat the unfurling of napkins as part of a predinner sideshow.)

If a gentleman briefly leaves the table during dinner, he leaves his napkin, loosely folded, in his chair. When he has finished his meal, however, he casually folds his napkin and places it to the side of his plate. He watches for his host or hostess to take the same action, which signals that the dinner party will be drawing to an end.

Even at the most elegant dinner party, a gentleman feels perfectly comfortable eating cold pick-up foods, such as asparagus spears, french fries, and fried chicken, with his fingers. However, he takes special care not to dribble the sauces over his shirtfront and the tablecloth.

———

If a gentleman discovers a raspberry seed or some other obstruction lodged between his teeth, he excuses himself and heads for the restroom.

———

At a cocktail party or at a seated dinner, if a gentleman discovers that he has put something unpleasant, or unpalatable, in his mouth, he gets rid of it in the most efficient way possible. In most cases, he simply uses his fingers or his fork. He works quickly and does not even attempt to disguise his actions behind a napkin.

———

Chapter Four

A GENTLEMAN SAYS THE RIGHT THING

There are certain questions that a gentleman never asks:

- "How do the two of you know each other?"
- "Why do I recognize your name?"
- "You don't remember me, do you?"
- "Would you mind if I look at the label?"
- "Are you going to eat all of that?"

———

A gentleman knows that "please" and "thank you" are still the magic words.

———

HOW TO START A CONVERSATION

At a party, a reception, or a business meeting, a gentleman strikes up a conversation with any pleasant person he encounters. To prevent awkwardness, however, he begins with positive, noncontroversial subject matter. He may say, "This is a nice party, isn't it?" or "Charlie has certainly done a good job of bringing this meeting together, hasn't he?" In every case, a gentleman begins by asking a question that does not bring the conversation around to himself. If the person standing next to him responds cordially, he continues with a few more questions until the conversation is under way. A gentleman knows that he is still testing the waters. Never, or at least not until the conversation is well under way, does he venture into uncertain territory, such as the lukewarm food on the buffet or the recent downslide of the company stock. Invariably, after he has made this sort of comment, a gentleman discovers that he is speaking to the hostess's sister or to the boss's son.

A gentleman does not make idle threats.

A gentleman does not brag.

A gentleman does not whine.

A gentleman knows how
to use a dictionary.

———

A gentleman accepts a compliment by
saying, "Thank you. It's nice of you to
tell me that." When a friend tells him,
"That's a good-looking tie, Jim," a
gentleman does not respond by saying,
"This old thing? I was almost ashamed to
bring it out." Such remarks imply
that the person paying the compliment
has questionable taste.

———

Whenever possible, a gentleman stays
away from sore subjects.

———

WHEN TO USE FIRST NAMES

Although the world at large is on a first-name basis today, a gentleman knows it is always safe, on first meeting, to address a new acquaintance as "Mr." or "Ms." He depends upon this guideline, especially if the new acquaintance is an older person or if he is dealing with his superior in a business environment. However, once "Ms. Jones" has told him, "Please, call me Mary," a gentleman concedes to her wish. Otherwise, he runs the risk of making her feel ill at ease.

In general, if a gentleman finds that a person of his own generation is referring to him as "Mr. Brown," he may logically assume that that person wishes to be referred to as "Mr." or "Ms." too. He does not attempt to force business acquaintances to act as if they were his personal friends.

How to End a Conversation

A gentleman recognizes that every conversation has its own natural rhythm. He is not being rude or inconsiderate when he attempts to bring any conversation—no matter how pleasant or how important—to a timely close.

When talking on the telephone, a gentleman accepts the responsibility for ending any conversation he has begun. When the conversation is taking place in his office, it is a gentleman's responsibility to bring the meeting to a close. In every case he states, as directly as possible, that it is time for the discussion to end; he does not allow the conversation to dawdle along uncomfortably. On the telephone, he may say something as simple as, "It's been very good talking to you, Jack. I hope we get to talk again soon." In person, he stands up, thanks his guest for meeting with him, and extends his hand for a handshake.

Even in a social situation, such as a cocktail party, a gentleman may end a conversation gracefully by saying, "It's been very pleasant talking to you, Mr. Grabbit. I'd like to freshen my drink. Would you care to walk over to the bar along with me?" In doing so, he provides himself with the opportunity to introduce Mr. Grabbit to other people. If Mr. Grabbit declines to accompany him to the bar, a gentleman says, "It really has been nice chatting with you. I hope we get to talk again soon."

When a gentleman initiates a telephone conversation, he knows it is his responsibility to end that conversation.

A gentleman gives direct answers,
especially to controversial questions.
Being direct, however, is not the same
thing as being blunt.

———

A gentleman never tells jokes that may
embarrass other people, even if those
other people are not in the room.

———

If a gentleman does not speak French, he
does not attempt to use French words.

———

When a gentleman quotes Shakespeare,
he does not give the name of the author.
If the quotation is not quite accurate, all
the better yet.

———

A gentleman does not curse in
the presence of women, children,
or older persons.

———

How to Respond to an Insult

When a gentleman has been subjected to a conscious insult, either in public or in private, his response is simple:

Because he is a gentleman, he says nothing at all.

A gentleman always
thinks before he speaks.

———

Unless he is teaching an English class, a gentleman does not correct another person's grammar. On the other hand, a gentleman monitors his own grammar scrupulously.

———

How to say, "I'm sorry."

Although he attempts at all times to be considerate of others, a gentleman sometimes makes mistakes. In such instances, he owns up to his failings and attempts to rectify the wrongdoing before matters grow any worse.

In making his apology, a gentleman is direct and to the point. If he has unintentionally made a remark that has hurt another person's feelings, he may say, "Sam, I'm afraid I said something rude to you last evening at the ball game when we were joking about the color of your shirt. I didn't mean to give offense." If his actions have made another person uncomfortable, he may say, for example, "The other night at the Wallaces', Sally, when I knocked your wineglass out of your hand, I felt like a klutz. I am sorry."

In making an apology, a gentleman does not downplay his error. Neither does he theatricalize it.

A gentleman apologizes when he is convinced that he has affronted another person. He does not offer an insincere apology if he has done nothing wrong. That sort of apology is a lie. It is an insult in and of itself.

A gentleman knows to keep an apology simple. He does not hold a grudge.

———

If an apology is sincerely offered, a gentleman accepts it with good grace. He does not pretend that the offense never existed, but he considers it past history and moves on.

———

A gentleman does not tell racist, sexist, or anti-gay jokes; neither does he laugh at them—even when he thinks only one other person is listening.

———

A gentleman never asks a woman if she is pregnant. He never asks, "Haven't you had that baby yet?"

———

When a gentleman inconveniences another person by asking him or her to shift so that he can move through a crowded room, he says, "Excuse me." He does not say, "I'm sorry," since there is no reason for him to apologize.

In fact, a gentleman never says, "I'm sorry," unless he has given offense.

———

How to Write
a Sympathy Note

It is appropriate for a gentleman to express sympathy upon the death of someone he has known, admired, or respected. He may express his sympathy to a friend who has lost a loved one, even if he never met the deceased person.

The simplest statements are the most eloquent. A gentleman might write, "I considered Harold a valuable and trusted friend. I will miss him very much." To comfort a friend he might write, "I know Harold's loss is a great blow to you. My thoughts are with you in this difficult time."

A gentleman never says, "Please let me know if there is anything I can do," leaving it up to the grieving person to ask for help. Instead he offers to supply a meal for the family, to run an errand, or to watch the house while the family is away.

How to make a complaint

There are times when a gentleman is perfectly justified in lodging a complaint. If he has received poor service, if he has been treated rudely, or if he has been the target of an undeserved affront, he has every right to make his displeasure known—not only for the sake of his bruised feelings, but also in hopes that the unpleasantness will not occur again.

A gentleman knows, however, that it is useless to make a complaint unless it is made to the right person. For instance, if a gentleman has received inferior service in a restaurant, he does not waste his breath complaining directly to the server, who may feel no compulsion to adjust his behavior. Instead, a gentleman expresses his concern to the manager or owner of the establishment. If he has the opportunity, he makes his complaint in person; otherwise, he makes a telephone call or he puts his concerns in writing.

When a gentleman makes a complaint, he describes specifically the reasons for his displeasure. He does not make threats. If he is poorly served at a restaurant or at any other establishment, he may choose to take his business there again. However, if the poor service continues after he has made his complaint, he does not continue to subject himself to further unpleasantness. He takes his business elsewhere.

A gentleman has definite beliefs, but he thinks before voicing his opinions. He recognizes that other people's beliefs are valid. He argues only over an issue that could save a life.

A gentleman never claims to have seen a movie he has not seen or to have read a book about which he has only read reviews. He knows how to say, "I haven't read [or seen] that yet, but from what I hear about it, it sounds very interesting. What did you think?"

————

If a gentleman is in financial distress, he does not bore other people with the details. If he is flush, he leaves that out of the conversation too.

————

Even if other people in the room are speaking in a foreign language, a gentleman is careful not to talk about them. He may not be able to speak Russian, but that does not mean the Russians are not fluent in English.

————

Chapter Five

A GENTLEMAN GIVES A PARTY

A gentleman does not give BYOB parties. Neither is he particularly fond of potluck dinners.

———

Whenever he can avoid it, a gentleman does not extend last-minute invitations. He has interesting friends, and he respects the fact that they have busy schedules.

———

A gentleman does not answer the phone during dinner. If he receives a call while he is entertaining, he politely asks if he may return it later.

———

WHAT EVERY GENTLEMAN HOST SHOULD KNOW

When he acts as host—in his own home or in a restaurant—a gentleman does everything in his power to entertain his guests. He knows that his goal is to put them at ease, not to impress them. He feels no need to serve the most extravagant hors d'oeuvres possible; neither does he feel compelled to take guests to the most expensive restaurant.

When his guests arrive, a gentleman greets them warmly and points them in the direction of food and drink. If he observes that a guest is not being included in the conversation, a gentleman introduces him to others and facilitates the conversation.

A gentleman host does not fret over broken glassware or scratches on the furniture. He accepts such irritations as a part of entertaining.

A gentleman makes sure that his invitation, whether it comes by telephone or by mail, provides all the necessary information. He gives the time, the date, and the location. He also lets people know what they are expected to wear.

———

If a guest offers to bring the wine or to help in some other way with the dinner menu, a gentleman may either accept or decline the offer. Either way, he says, "Thank you," and means it.

———

A gentleman host uses his good china. If a piece is broken accidentally, he does not make a scene, neither does he accept a guest's offer to pay for its replacement.

———

If a guest arrives with an unexpected dish, a gentleman serves it. He need not, however, open a bottle of unexpected wine, especially if it is not appropriate for the food being served.

————

If a gentleman is giving an extremely intimate dinner party—for only one or two guests—he may ask his guests to join him in the kitchen as he finishes the dinner preparations. If his kitchen is small, they may stand in the door so that he can join in the conversation.

————

A gentleman sometimes discovers that he has made the mistake of inviting ill-mannered people into his home. He does not attempt to reform such people's behavior. Instead, he does not invite them back to his home.

————

THE ART OF THE SOCIAL KISS

A gentleman knows that a social kiss is not an erotic experience. It expresses the mildest sort of affection. It happens quickly and means hardly more than a handshake. A social kiss is shared only among people who are already friends. It is never offered in a business situation.

A gentleman always waits for the woman to initiate a social kiss. If she leans toward him, he turns his cheek toward her lips, and she graces him with a light, brushing kiss. She does not linger in giving the kiss. Neither does he dawdle in accepting it. He may place one hand on her shoulder.

If a woman's lipstick leaves a smudge on a gentleman's face, he does not wipe it away in her presence. Instead, he bears it, even if briefly, as a badge of honor, wiping it away later with his handkerchief.

A gentleman always sets the table
before his guests arrive.

———

When liquor is being served, a gentleman
host is always alert to the possibility that
some guests may overindulge. In such
cases he does not allow them to drive.
He arranges for them to be driven
home by a sober friend, or he calls
a cab. If he feels he must take away a
guest's car keys, he does so.

———

If a gentleman wants his guests to leave,
he puts the liquor away.

———

When a gentleman takes a gift to a
party, unless it is a baby or wedding
shower, he does not assume that it will
be opened in his presence.

———

How to set up a bar

A gentleman does not stock his bar in order to impress people. He stocks his bar with the libations people actually want to drink. For even the largest, most eclectic group, a choice of scotch, vodka, gin, white wine, and in the South, bourbon, will suffice. What is more, his guests will find themselves much less confused.

In every case, a gentleman makes sure to have ample ice, and he offers a variety of mixers, not just for the pleasure of his drinker friends, but out of consideration for his teetotaling guests as well. Quality, a gentleman knows, is always more important than quirkiness.

A gentleman knows that his bar is never complete without sliced limes and lemons, a jigger, a stirrer, and a tall stack of hand-ironed, starched cotton cocktail napkins.

How to seat a table

If a gentleman entertains—whether in his home or in a public place—the moment will come when he will be expected to "seat" a table. At that moment he, as a host, will be asked to decide where each of his guests will sit during the meal ahead of them. A gentleman takes this obligation seriously, knowing that his decision will make or break the evening. He attempts to seat compatible guests beside each another, but he never seats a couple—whether they are married, long-standing lovers, or on a first date—side by side. His goal is to create a mix of guests who will ask each other questions, generating lively conversation.

If there is a guest of honor, that person is always given the best seat. At a banquet, for example, the honored guest is given the seat with the best view of the room. In a

private home, the guest of honor is seated
at the host's right hand or, better yet,
between two particularly congenial guests.

Meanwhile, a gentleman-host reserves
for himself the least desirable seat. For
instance, at a formal dinner where there
are to be speeches, the host takes the seat
with the poorest view of the podium. His
compensatory reward comes from
watching the happy faces of his
handsomely entertained guests.

If a gentleman prefers to prepare the
dinner himself, he tells his guests and
gratefully declines their offers for help. If
he would like their assistance, however,
he accepts the offers. If an offer is not
made, he may still ask for help in small
chores, such as opening the wine or
filling the glasses with ice.

How to set a dinner table

A gentleman knows how to set an elegant, if rudimentary, dinner table. The basic equipment is arranged in this manner:

When Salad is served as a First Course

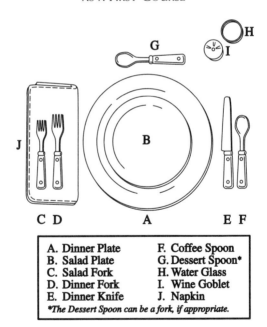

A. Dinner Plate
B. Salad Plate
C. Salad Fork
D. Dinner Fork
E. Dinner Knife
F. Coffee Spoon
G. Dessert Spoon*
H. Water Glass
I. Wine Goblet
J. Napkin

The Dessert Spoon can be a fork, if appropriate.

WHEN SALAD IS SERVED

ALONG WITH THE ENTRÉE

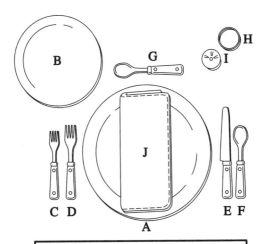

A. Dinner Plate	F. Coffee Spoon
B. Salad Plate	G. Dessert Spoon*
C. Salad Fork	H. Water Glass
D. Dinner Fork	I. Wine Goblet
E. Dinner Knife	J. Napkin

The Dessert Spoon can be a fork, if appropriate.

HOW TO SERVE DINNER

Before a gentleman's guests arrive, he has already placed the dinner plates, flatware, and glasses on the table. Once the guests have chatted for a bit, and have perhaps had a drink of some sort, he suggests that they proceed to the table. Thereafter, the procedure is as follows:

- The guests take their places.
- If a gentleman is serving a salad, he places the salad plates directly on the dinner plates (which have already been set.)
- When the guests have finished their salads, a gentleman removes the salad plates. If he plans to serve the dinner plates in the kitchen, he takes them away at the same time. The salad forks remain on the guests' plates.
- Either a gentleman serves the dinner plates in the kitchen, or he brings out

the main course and its side dishes to the table, where the guests serve themselves.

- When guests have finished the main course, with second helpings if they are offered, a gentleman takes away the dinner plates along with the dinner forks and knives.

- A gentleman serves dessert. If he has not already placed the dessert forks or spoons on the table, he may bring them out along with the dessert itself. If there is coffee, he serves it now.

If the dinner conversation continues after the guests have finished their desserts, a gentleman takes the empty plates away and pours more coffee. He never, never rushes his friends to leave the table after a satisfying meal.

If a gentleman guest breaks a piece of china or glassware when being entertained at another person's home (and it *does* happen—not all gentleman are graceful), he apologizes. Instead of offering to pay for its replacement, however, he replaces the broken item itself.

———

If a guest offers to help clean up after the party, a gentleman may either accept or decline the offer. However, he has no reason to expect that such an offer will be made. From start-to-finish, hosting a party is a one-man job.

———

Chapter Six

A GENTLEMAN GOES
TO A PARTY

A gentleman does not turn
down invitations. He *never* waits for
something better to turn up.

―――

A gentleman is never the last to leave a
party. Neither, if he can possibly help it,
is he the first to arrive.

―――

A gentleman does not make long-
distance calls from other people's houses
unless he uses a credit card.

―――

How to Respond to an Invitation

A gentleman wastes no time in responding to an invitation. If he sees the letters RSVP (an abbreviation for the French equivalent of "Please reply"), he is obligated to respond, either by telephone or in writing. An RSVP requires that he reply whether or not he plans to attend the event in question. If the directive is "Regrets only," he need inform his host or hostess only if he does *not* plan to show up. A gentleman understands that it is vastly inconsiderate for him not to make his intentions known.

If a gentleman must decline an invitation, he gives a straightforward reason for doing so. "I have a prior engagement," "I will have guests from out of town," and "I will be away on vacation" are all perfectly acceptable explanations.

A gentleman does not lay down conditions for his accepting an invitation. He does not ask, "What will you be serving?" or "Who else is going to be there?" He accepts the invitation gladly and proves to himself that because he is a gentleman, he can have a good time in any company, at any time.

If an invitation is marked "RSVP," a gentleman always responds, making it clear whether or not he expects to attend the event.

———

When a gentleman discovers that he can attend a party for which he has already refused an invitation, he calls his host or hostess and asks if he may attend.

———

A gentleman understands the dress code provided on his party invitation. "Casual" varies with the season: shorts and a polo shirt for summer, jeans and a sweater for winter. "Business casual" suggests an open shirt and a sports jacket. "Semi-formal" requires a dark suit and tie. "Black tie" dictates a dinner jacket and its necessary accouterments: a vest or cummerbund, cufflinks and studs, a good white shirt, and brightly polished black shoes. "White tie" demands the gentleman's ultimate regalia, complete with tailcoat and patent leather dancing shoes.

———

A gentleman does not lean back in his chair.

———

Once a gentleman discovers that he must decline an invitation that he has already accepted, he promptly lets his host or hostess know. He gives a frank description of the reasons for his change of plan and offers a sincere apology.

———

When a gentleman receives a number of invitations on his answering machine he always accepts the first one. Even in the world of voice mail, it is rude to weigh one invitation against another. A gentleman never waits for something better to come along.

———

If an invitation says, "Regrets only," a gentleman lets the host or hostess know that he does *not* plan to attend.

———

How to be a Guest
at a Party

A gentleman knows that accepting an invitation is like signing a business contract. His host promises to entertain the guests, and he agrees to do his part to make the event a success.

He arrives on time—not early and not more than fifteen minutes late. He participates in the activities that have been planned, and he makes pleasant conversation with the other guests. He does not gorge himself at the dinner table, although he takes a second helping when it is offered. He does not overindulge at the bar.

When the party is winding down, he exits with efficient grace. He thanks his host or hostess and says good-bye to any new friends he may have made.

A gentleman does not take a date to a party unless he is certain he is expected to do so. If his invitation is not addressed to him "and guest," he does not have the license to bring a guest.

———

When a gentleman is offered a name tag, he puts it on.

———

At a party a gentleman never spends all his time talking to one person. He is always excited to meet as many people as possible, and he assumes that a great many people will enjoy meeting him too.

———

If a gentleman does not see an ashtray, he does not smoke—and he does not ask if he may do so. If he must light up he steps outside.

———

A gentleman uses a coaster.

———

A gentleman feels free to use the hand towel in the powder room. He does not attempt to refold it. Otherwise, other guests will not know it has been used.

———

A gentleman asks for seconds when they are offered. If he has any good sense, however, he will never choose to be seen eating, or drinking, alone.

———

WHEN TO TAKE A GIFT

When a gentleman is invited to someone's home—for dinner, a holiday party, or for an overnight visit—he takes a gift. For a dinner party, he takes a bouquet of flowers or a bottle of wine (unchilled, so that the host or hostess knows that it is a *gift*, and is not intended to accompany dinner). For a holiday party, he takes a jar of mustard, some jam, a bottle of good whiskey, a tin of nuts, or a bag of coffee beans. If he is invited for a more extended stay—a single night or longer—a gentleman takes a more substantial gift, such as cloth cocktail napkins, an extra corkscrew, or a useful kitchen gadget.

A gentleman always presents his gift directly to his host or hostess. Even though he takes a gift a gentleman also sends a thank-you note at his first opportunity.

How to make a toast

Over the course of his life, a gentleman will probably be invited to any number of wedding receptions, anniversary dinners, birthday parties, and other events. At some time, almost inevitably, he will be asked to make a toast, and if he is asked, he must not refuse. However, he need not attempt to give an after-dinner speech or perform a comedy routine. His tribute may be something as simple as "Joe, I'm proud to call you my friend." He may choose to share some memory of his friendship with the honoree, or if he is confident of his skill as a humorist, he may toss off a lighthearted quip. In no case does he attempt to embarrass the guest of honor. Neither does he ramble on at any length. A gentleman remembers that because toasts usually come late in the evening, the wisest course is always to be succinct.

If a toast is being made, a gentleman, even if he is a teetotaler, always raises his glass. He never toasts with an empty glass. Even a glass of water, raised in the right spirit, expresses a wish for good luck.

———

Even if a gentleman has brought a bottle of wine to dinner, he still writes a thank-you note.

———

After a toast has been made, a gentleman clinks his glass against any other glass that is extended toward his own.

———

A gentleman is cordial and friendly to the bartenders at a private party. However, he is not required to leave tips for them. That is the responsibility of the host.

———

WHEN TO SEND
A THANK-YOU NOTE

A gentleman always sends a thank-you
note. Whether he brought flowers or a
casserole to a potluck dinner, he is still
grateful. Even if he brings a bottle of wine,
he still writes a note. (The flowers say,
"Thank you for inviting me." The note
says, "Thank you, I had a good time.") It is
not the same thing.) If he has brought
flowers or wine, the note does not have to
be sent immediately. If the evening is
boring, or if he leaves early, he can always
say something like, "I had such fun pausing
with you before the marathon of yet
another busy weekend." Or he can say,
"Dinner was so good, I tried a little bit of
everything."

The host or hostess need not reply to a
thank-you note.

A gentleman has never been seated
beside a boring person at dinner. Neither
has he ever been seated beside a person
who has been bored.

———

A gentleman may not be able to dance
a samba, but he should be capable of
a fox-trot, which is almost
like not dancing at all.

———

Unless he is asked, a gentleman does
not operate another person's sound
system. Neither does he touch another
person's CDs.

———

A GENTLEMAN GOES TO A PARTY

If a gentleman arrives at a private party and discovers that valet parking has been provided, he pulls into line and waits his turn. When he pulls up to the door of the house, he allows the parking attendant to open the car doors—both for the gentleman's guests and for the gentleman himself. The gentleman does not forget to leave the keys in the ignition. He makes sure to have his tip money ready at the end of the evening.

———

A gentleman always carries dollar bills in his pocket. He never knows when he may need to tip a doorman, a maître d', or a parking attendant. He even carries a few extra singles to lend to other gentlemen or ladies who may be caught unprepared.

———

Chapter Seven

A GENTLEMAN AND HIS FRIENDS

A gentleman never gets so big that he can feel free to say or do things that make other people feel small.

———

A gentleman does not lend more money than he can afford to spare. He does not borrow more money than he can afford to pay back.

———

A gentleman does not shout at deaf people or at people who are blind.

———

How to make an introduction

Even in our increasingly casual society, a gentleman respects the time-honored traditions surrounding social introductions:

- A younger person is always introduced *to* an older person. For example, when Larry Lyons, who is in his twenties, is introduced to Mr. Allgood, who is in his fifties, a gentleman says, "Mr. Allgood, I'd like you to meet Larry Lyons." Even if a younger woman is being introduced to an older man, a gentleman makes sure to say the older person's name first.

- When a gentleman introduces a man and a woman who are of essentially the same age, he introduces the man *to* the woman. Thus, if his friends Sally Baldwin and Larry Lyons do not know each other, a gentleman introduces them by saying, "Sally, this is my friend, Larry Lyons." Then a gentleman turns to Larry and says, "Larry, this is Sally Baldwin."

- In all cases, a gentleman feels free to add some detail to stimulate conversation. He might, for example, say, "Mr. Allgood, Larry is one of my good friends from law school." Or, "Sally, you may have heard me talk about Larry. We went to the Mozart concert last week."

- A gentleman makes every effort to pronounce names clearly. If it is convenient, he repeats the names at some not-too-distant point in the conversation.

Even if he is uncertain of the protocol of the moment, however, a gentleman always does his best to make an introduction. Even if he makes a small mistake, he has not committed the more serious mistake of being rude.

A gentleman never assumes anybody knows anybody else. He always makes introductions. He is ready to give his own name.

———

A gentleman stands up when he is introduced.

———

When a gentleman realizes that another gentleman has neglected to close his fly, he tells him about it, even in a crowded room.

———

When a gentleman realizes that his fly is open, he zips up—on the spot, if convenient. Never does an open fly require an apology.

———

HOW TO DEAL WITH NONDRINKERS

Any gentleman may have friends who do not drink alcohol. Whatever the reason for that choice—religious belief, health, or addiction—a gentleman respects it. He does not pressure anyone to drink; neither does he ask probing questions. He makes certain that his nondrinking friends have plenty of appealing nonalcoholic options.

If a gentleman chooses not to drink alcohol, he does not impose that decision on other people. If he is offered a cocktail, he may say, "Thanks, but I don't drink alcohol. I'd like a soda or some sparkling water—whatever you have handy." He offers no further explanation.

HOW TO SHAKE HANDS

A gentleman may feel free to shake hands with anyone to whom he is introduced, or with any acquaintance he encounters in a social situation, whether at a party, in a theater lobby, or in an aisle at church. However, a gentleman does respect certain guidelines. When he is introduced to an older person or to a dignitary, a gentleman does not extend his hand first. Instead, he waits until a handshake is offered. Then he firmly grasps the extended hand, just below the knuckles, and gives it a couple of modest pumps. He uses a light, painless grip and lets go immediately after the handshake is finished.

A gentleman never extends his hand to a woman first. It is always her prerogative to decide if she wishes to shake hands. In any case, when shaking hands with a woman, a gentleman is wise to give her hand a quick, gentle press rather than a full-fledged up-and-down pump. If a lady does not extend her hand, a gentleman simply nods his head.

A gentleman never refuses to shake a hand that is extended to him. Such a refusal is the most blatant insult possible in the business or the social world.

When a gentleman is in the company of
a woman—whether she is his mother,
his wife, his lover, his boss, or his
friend—and they are walking
through a crowded room,
he walks slightly behind her.

————

A gentleman does not crash parties.

————

A gentleman is always on time for
social occasions. If there will be
a cocktail hour prior to a seated dinner,
he may arrive as much as a half hour
late. However, if he has been invited for
dinner only, and if he is running more
than fifteen minutes late, he phones
ahead and asks his host or hostess to
begin the meal without him.

————

When to Send Flowers

A gentleman feels free to send flowers to mark almost any occasion, happy or sad. Flowers may celebrate an anniversary, a birthday, a holiday, a promotion, the birth of a baby, or any other joyful moment in life. They are the perfect means of thanking a host or hostess, and they may be sent either before or after the party. On the other hand, flowers may also be sent to comfort a grieving family or to brighten a sick person's room. They may be sent to say "I'm sorry" when a gentleman has been guilty of an unintentional affront.

At the same time, a gentleman knows that there are a few occasions when flowers—or at least certain types of flowers—are not the right gesture. If a mourning family has asked that no flowers be sent to a funeral, a gentleman sends none. He does not send flowers to his secretary—or to any other coworker—at her home. Instead he has an arrangement of cut flowers or, better yet, a hardy green plant delivered to her desk.

Finally, a gentleman knows that unless a woman is a grandmother of the bride, he never sends a corsage.

When there is a woman on the premises—or if there is any likelihood a woman will arrive soon—a gentleman always puts the toilet lid down.

———

In the morning, a gentleman always offers to get up and make the coffee.

———

How to be a houseguest

As a guest in a private home a gentleman treats his host's furniture and other belongings with the greatest care, even more carefully than if they were his own.

If there are servants and some special service is done for him, or if he stays any great length of time, he shows his gratitude by leaving a thank-you tip.

In every case, a gentleman attempts to fit into the household routine. He rises and retires according to the household schedule. He eats what is served and does not complain. He makes his bed in the morning, and he disposes of damp towels as he is instructed.

Most important, he sticks to his arrival and departure plans. When his visit is over, he checks his room to make sure he has packed all his belongings. He leaves nothing but pleasant memories behind.

How to deal with
unmarried couples

A gentleman may have many friends and acquaintances who live together in nontraditional relationships. If a gentleman decides to make these people a part of his life, he accepts them as they are, recognizing that their private life is their business and no one else's. If he does not approve of their behavior, he does not preach to them. Instead, he associates with them as seldom as possible.

In no case does he mention their relationship when introducing them to other people. For example, a gentleman does not say, "This is Mary Brown, and this is her live-in boyfriend [or "her significant other" or "the father of her child"], Sam Jones." Instead, he says, "I'd like you to meet my friends Mary Brown and Sam Jones." Especially in the case of gay or lesbian couples, a gentleman avoids attempting to define the couple's relationship to outsiders. He will be wise to say, "Please meet Bob Grainger and Keith Harris," or "Please meet Kate Williams and Helen Thompson," and leave it at that.

If the couple feels the need to provide any further details about their living arrangement, they may do so, although in most cases they will be telling people more than they really need or want to know.

In written correspondence with Mary and Sam, a gentleman addresses the envelope to "Ms. Mary Brown and Mr. Sam Jones." A letter to Bob and Keith would be addressed to "Mr. Bob Grainger and Mr. Keith Harris." Kate and Helen's letter would go to "Ms. Helen Thompson and Ms. Kate Williams," listing them in alphabetical order.

HOW TO DEAL WITH DIVORCED FRIENDS

A gentleman regrets seeing any loving relationship break up, especially if he considers both persons to be his friends. However, his regret is for their pain, not for his own. He does not take sides in their marital strife; he does not carry tales back and forth between the opposing camps.

If his friends are recently divorced, a gentleman does not attempt to put them in situations—a small dinner party, for example—where they will be forced to encounter each other. He tries to maintain communication with both parties, but he understands that he is now friends with *two people*, not with a couple. Maintaining these friendships may require twice as much effort—and twice as much time.

After a reasonable amount of time has passed, however, a gentleman may feel free to include both friends in the same event, especially when a good many other people are involved. To forestall any anxiety, though, he is thoughtful enough to make sure both parties are informed ahead of time. He also makes sure that his guest list includes other single people, so that the divorced person does not feel like a fifth wheel.

A gentleman may say to Betsy, formerly married to Tom, "It's going to be fun, Betsy. I've invited Jim and Marcia, and Bob, Jim, Gloria, Ted and Vivian. I'm going to ask Tom too."

Because a gentleman's friends are well-mannered people, they would never ask him for such information ahead of time. However, a gentleman understands if, given the circumstances, they choose to decline his invitation. Only in such extraordinary circumstances, after all, would a well-mannered person ever decline.

In matters of politics or religion, a gentleman does not assume that everyone believes what he believes.

———

If a gentleman says he will call, he lives up to his word.

———

A gentleman is considerate of the special needs of senior citizens and physically challenged people. For example, if he encounters a blind person who seems confused by a busy street corner, he asks, "May I help you across to the sidewalk?" If the offer is accepted, the gentleman provides a helpful hand. If the offer is declined, he maintains his distance, keeping a watchful eye.

———

A gentleman does not make phone calls to anyone during the dinner hour.

———

On a rainy day, a gentleman will extend a hand to help anyone over a mud puddle.

———

A gentleman is not afraid to carry breath mints. Neither is he reluctant to offer them to other people.

———

If a gentleman must park his own car at a restaurant, or any other place of entertainment, he offers to let his passengers out at the door.

———

A gentleman is perfectly willing to accept "No." for an answer—the *first* time he hears it.

———

A gentleman never attempts to make a last-minute date. However, if a couple of good tickets fall into his hands by happenstance, he does not neglect the opportunity to share them with someone whose company he enjoys.

———

A gentleman breaks a date only for reasons of sickness, death, or natural disaster. If he must cancel his plans, he does so with as much advance warning as possible.

Chapter Eight

A GENTLEMAN GOES TO THE OFFICE

A gentleman may choose to carry work home from the office. He does not, however, assume that his fellow employees will do the same.

———

If a gentleman is in the position to supervise the work of other people in his office, he does not attempt to dictate. Instead, he directs.

———

A gentleman never writes personal letters on his business stationery.

———

THE ETIQUETTE OF THE ANSWERING MACHINE

A gentleman never assumes that anyone recognizes his voice on an answering machine microcassette tape. He speaks clearly, identifies himself, and leaves his phone number. Better yet, he speaks slowly and gives the number twice. In no case, does a gentleman hog the tape. He leaves his message and then gets on with his life. If he needs to have a conversation, he can have one over dinner.

When a gentleman's phone message is not returned in a timely fashion and a deadline is involved, he calls back and if necessary, leaves a second message. At this point, it is the other person's responsibility to return the call.

If a gentleman receives a message that involves a deadline, like a dinner invitation, he returns the message promptly.

When a gentleman is asked to take a message for a fellow employee, he does so. He makes certain that he takes the message accurately, and he remembers to deliver it.

———

A gentleman does not barge into another person's office, even if the door has been left open.

———

If a gentleman works in an open office space, he remembers that others can overhear his conversations. He speaks in a quiet tone of voice. He does not shout across the office. Neither does he laugh raucously while others are busy working.

———

If a gentleman borrows a pen from a fellow employee, he returns it promptly. He does not lose the cap.

———

A GENTLEMAN AND HIS BOSS

Even in today's egalitarian society, a gentleman remembers that in some situations, there still is a chain of command. He may be on a first-name basis with his employer, and they may enjoy an occasional golf game together, but he still remembers who is in charge in the office. He accepts his work assignments with good grace unless they are in some way repellent to him. If a gentleman feels the need to deny a request from his boss, he gives his reasons for doing so, with frankness and without delay.

In semisocial situations, such as having a casual drink after work, a gentleman accepts without resistance his boss's offer to pick up the tab—even if his boss is a woman. During the holidays, if his boss gives him a present, a gentleman accepts it and expresses his gratitude. He understands that his boss does not expect a gift in return. Such a present acknowledges a job well done; it does not suggest an exchange between friends.

If a gentleman is entertained in his boss's home, he treats his boss and his boss's spouse just as he would treat any other host and hostess. He takes a small gift if it seems appropriate, and he always writes a thank-you note. Even if the occasion was purely an office party, a gentleman's boss has extended the kindness of inviting outsiders into his home.

A gentleman does not lie on his résumé.

―――

On a job interview, a gentleman dresses as he would for a day at the office. In that way he makes it clear that he understands the nature of the business.

―――

After a job interview, a gentleman writes a thank-you note.

―――

When a gentleman resigns from his job, he does not burn bridges.

―――

A gentleman always restocks the copy machine with paper.

―――

A GENTLEMAN AND HIS SECRETARY

A gentleman treats his secretary/ administrative assistant, and any other members of his staff, with all the respect due a valued coworker and a fellow human being. He makes his expectations clearly known, and he readily expresses his gratitude for a job well done.

He is careful to keep the line clearly drawn between his personal and professional lives. If his level of trust is great enough, he may ask his secretary to make his bank deposit for him. However, unless she is extremely well paid and functions as his personal assistant, he does not ask her to balance his checkbook or pay his bills. He may ask her to set up a business lunch. He does not ask her to set up a date.

He may give her a gift on special occasions—such as a work anniversary, her birthday, or a holiday—but he is always wise to stick with flowers, a book, or some other impersonal item. He does not expect her to give him a gift in return.

No matter how many years the two of them have worked together, and no matter how pressing the deadlines of their work, a gentleman does not neglect to tell his secretary, "Thank you." Even if he is only asking her to make photocopies, he does not forget to say, "Please."

If a gentleman realizes that he is going to be more than five minutes late for a business appointment, he telephones ahead.

When leaving on a business trip with other colleagues, a gentleman shows up on time.

———

If a gentleman is asked whether he wishes to share a hotel room while on a business trip, he makes his preference known. If company policy requires sharing rooms, he behaves courteously and considerately to his roommate.

———

On a business trip a gentleman does not abuse the privileges of his expense account.

———

When a gentleman entertains a business client, it is his responsibility to pick up the tab.

———

A gentleman realizes that a personal E-mail is like a personal phone call. He does not interrupt the workday with personal business unless an emergency or a dire social crisis is involved.

———

A gentleman does not fire off angry E-mails. Once they have been sent, he knows there is no taking them back.

———

A gentleman always keeps business cards in his desk and his briefcase. If a new business acquaintance offers him a card, he treats it with respect, slipping it into his pocket or his wallet. He does not leave it behind, and he does not use it to clean his fingernails.

———

A gentleman keeps his address book up to date.

———

THE ETIQUETTE OF E-MAIL

A gentleman treats E-mail like any other written correspondence. He expresses himself clearly and concisely. He does not send lengthy sequences of short, inconsequential messages that clutter up the recipient's E-mail directory. He indicates the topic of his correspondence in the "Subject" line of his E-mail, so that the recipient can identify it in his or her directory.

If a gentleman is sending a copy of his E-mail to a second correspondent, he indicates that he is sending a copy in the same way that he would use "cc:" at the bottom of a letter. He knows E-mail is never completely private, since it is read on a computer screen and often in an office environment. To save embarrassment to himself and to his correspondent, he is discreet about the messages he sends.

THE ETIQUETTE OF THE OFFICE BREAK ROOM

Even if a gentleman is not meticulous about how he behaves in his own kitchen, he maintains higher standards in the office break room or the communal kitchen. He never leaves his dirty coffee cup, his dirty dishes, or his dirty silverware in the sink. If there is no dishwasher, he washes his own dishes. He also dries them and puts them away. He does not leave his leftovers in the office refrigerator for an excessively long time. And he never assumes that he has an automatic right to sample anything left in the refrigerator by a fellow employee.

At the office, as at home, a gentleman always refills the ice trays.

————

A gentleman learns the names of receptionists, administrative assistants, and secretaries at the offices where he makes frequent calls. He thanks them for their assistance as often as possible.

————

A gentleman always offers to change the water cooler tank.

————

A gentleman never asks a coworker, especially not one of his employees, to make the coffee. If he is a coffee drinker, he learns how to operate the coffeemaker himself.

————

When a gentleman changes his business address or phone number, he informs his business associates as quickly as possible.

———

A gentleman shares his home phone number only with those business associates who really need it. Except in extraordinary circumstances, he does not divulge the home phone numbers of people who work with him.

———

If a gentleman discovers, during a large business meeting, that he needs to use the bathroom, he leaves the room quietly. He does not need to announce where he is going or when he plans to return. When he must leave a small meeting, he excuses himself, saying, "I'll be back in a few minutes."

———

Chapter Nine

A GENTLEMAN GETS EQUIPPED

A gentleman reads a daily newspaper, preferably the *New York Times*, at least three times a week.

———

A gentleman keeps an umbrella in his car.

———

A gentleman knows how to sew on a button. In his bathroom cabinet and in his desk at the office, he keeps a needle and thread.

———

A gentleman never runs out
of toilet paper.

———

If a gentleman can afford it, he has
someone else clean his house for him.

———

A gentleman chooses a dry cleaner
carefully. The people behind the counter
know his name. They also know what
kind of starch he likes.

———

A gentleman keeps a good quality
corkscrew in his kitchen drawer.

———

A gentleman always carries a
handkerchief. Because it is always clean,
he readily lends it to others.

———

A CHECKLIST FOR A GENTLEMAN'S LINENS

Although he may not use them himself every day, a gentleman has on hand:

- At least a half dozen heavy white cotton dinner napkins. (Even if he has dinnerware only for four, he is wise to have a couple of extra napkins on hand, in case of spills and so that he can use one to line the bread basket.)
- At least a half dozen heavy white cotton cocktail napkins.
- A couple of spare packs of heavy paper cocktail napkins.
- A half dozen heavy cotton kitchen towels. (Otherwise, he will find himself using his dinner napkins to wipe up messes in the kitchen.)

In the bathroom, in the cabinet under the sink, he keeps:

- At least two good fluffy cotton towels that he does not use every day. (Even an unexpected overnight guest deserves a fresh towel.)
- At least two washcloths that match his towels.
- At least two hand towels for guests to use. (These should not be the same ones he uses every morning to wipe his face after shaving.)

A gentleman owns cloth napkins.

———

A gentleman always writes in either black or blue-black ink. He never uses a ballpoint pen.

———

A gentleman always has a box of good quality, heavy cardboard correspondence cards for his informal correspondence—thank-you notes, sympathy notes, replies to formal invitations, even the occasional billet-doux. They may be plain, imprinted, or engraved with his name.

———

A gentleman maintains a stock of good quality writing papers for his personal use. For most social correspondence he uses the readily available standard-size 7¼" x 10½" paper known as "monarch sheets."

———

A gentleman uses his personal stationery to write thank-you notes. If he has to say, "I'm sorry," he uses the phone.

———

A CHECKLIST FOR A GENTLEMAN'S GLASSWARE

Because he is likely to entertain with some frequency, and because things do get broken, a gentleman keeps a good supply of glassware. Because he is likely to entertain other gentlemen, he goes for unfussy, hard-to-break patterns that rest comfortably in the hand.

On his glassware shelf he keeps:

- At least eight old-fashioned glasses, for whiskey and other on-the-rocks drinks. (They can also be used for fruit juice at breakfast.)
- At least eight double old-fashioned glasses, for mixed drinks, such as vodka and tonic. (They also serve perfectly well for sodas and iced tea.)
- At least eight large multipurpose wineglasses. (The bubble shape,

although intended primarily for red wine, will work for almost anything. What's more, even if a gentleman does not drink wine, they are great for desserts, like ice cream with a dribble of Hershey's chocolate sauce.)

- A half dozen brandy snifters if he is the brandy-drinking sort.

A gentleman does not waste his money on pilsner glasses for beer. He is content to drink his beer from a can, as long as he uses a cocktail napkin.

A Gentleman's Checklist for China

Even if he entertains only on the rarest of occasions, a gentleman is equipped with everything necessary to set a basic dinner table. In his kitchen cabinets, he has available:

- At least four dinner plates that match. (Heavy pottery or white dishwasher-safe bistro-style plates are fine. They are also microwave safe.)
- At least four salad plates that look nice with the dinner plates. (They need not match one another, but they must look good together on the same table.)
- At least four soup bowls that complement the dinner plates. (Hearty ones, large enough for chili or beef stew, are recommended.)
- At least four matching cups and saucers.

- Flatware (probably stainless) for four, including:
  - Four knives
  - Four dinner forks
  - Four salad forks
  - Four soup spoons
  - Four coffee spoons

A gentleman makes sure that all his dinnerware is unchipped and clean before he puts it on the table. Even if his flatware has been through the dishwasher, he rubs it with a cloth before setting the table so that it takes on a little shine.

A gentleman has a rudimentary
knowledge of at least
one foreign language.

———

A gentleman makes a will, both for his
own peace of mind and out of
consideration for others.

———

A gentleman considers it a wise
investment to pay for dancing lessons.

———

A gentleman knows how and under
what circumstances to send flowers.

———

Chapter Ten

EXTREME ETIQUETTE

A Gentleman Faces the Really Big Challenges

Meeting Royalty

There is nothing casual about an encounter with royalty. If a gentleman is presented to the queen of England, for example, he must wait for her to initiate any conversation, and he must not touch her unless she extends her hand first. He refers to her as "Ma'am," allows her to ask all the questions, and waits for her to bring the conversation to a close.

If a gentleman is a citizen of the United States, he does not bow or even nod his head to another country's ruler.

If he is wearing a hat, of course, he removes it as a gesture of respect.

An invitation to the White House

If a gentleman is invited to the White House, for any occasion, he must not refuse. Only in the case of a death in the family or a serious illness may he decline.

If the invitation is a formal one (engraved on heavy paper, complete with the presidential seal), a gentleman must respond to it formally, writing by hand. If the invitation is more casual, perhaps a telephone call from the president's secretary or an assistant to the first lady, a gentleman responds in kind.

If the invitation is for a daytime event, such as a luncheon, a gentleman wears a dark suit. If the occasion is a dinner or some other evening event, the gentleman wears black tie.

Smoking is not allowed.

MEETING THE PRESIDENT

Preparing to meet the president in a receiving line, a gentleman goes *ahead* of the woman who is his companion. He waits for the president to initiate a handshake and any passing conversation. A gentleman refers to the president as "Sir" (or someday, as "Ma'am") or as "Mr. President" ("Madame President").

The president's spouse is referred to by his or her married name, "Mrs. Coolidge," for example, or "Mr. Coolidge."

As long as the president is standing, everyone else in the room remains standing as well.

How to kiss a lady's hand

If he travels in Europe, a gentleman may find himself expected to kiss a lady's hand. It is not, however, the sort of thing that happens with any frequency in the United States any more.

Nevertheless, if a woman should extend her hand to a gentleman, palm down and extended out before her so that it is clear a handshake is not what she had in mind, the gentleman simply places his lips lightly against her skin, presses her fingers for a second, and then allows her to pull her hand away.

The action, of course, requires that a gentleman bow from the waist.

AN AUDIENCE
WITH THE POPE

To obtain an audience with the pope,
a gentleman must have excellent
connections in the Catholic church. If the
request is granted, he will receive a ticket
for an audience at a specific time at
the Vatican.

A gentleman wears his most
businesslike, most dignified suit.

Everyone stands as the pope enters and
leaves the audience chamber. The service
will consist of a brief sermon by the pope
followed by a blessing. Even non-Catholics
are expected to kneel and stand along with
the rest of the congregation. However,
they need not cross themselves. If there is
time, the pope may greet the visitors
individually. The pope is referred to as
"Your Holiness."

MEETING OTHER
PUBLIC FIGURES

Whenever a gentleman is given the opportunity to meet a celebrity—from the realms of sports, politics, or the arts—he treats that person with simple respect. Fawning adulation is not necessary.

As public figures, most celebrities feel a certain responsibility to sign autographs or accept compliments from strangers. However, a gentleman would never intrude on a celebrity—or anyone else whom he does not know, for that matter—during an intimate dinner or a private conversation.

If the gentleman feels he must make the most of the moment, he begins by saying, "Excuse me." He keeps the encounter brief and non-confrontational. When it is finished, he says, "Thank you for your time."

OTHER FORMS OF ADDRESS
FOR DIGNITARIES

THE VICE PRESIDENT

"Mr. (Madame) Vice President"

or "Sir (Madame)"

A UNITED STATES SENATOR

"Senator _____"

A MEMBER OF THE HOUSE OF

REPRESENTATIVES

"Representative _____"

GOVERNOR OF A STATE

"Governor _____"

AN EPISCOPAL OR ROMAN CATHOLIC BISHOP

"Bishop _____"

A ROMAN CATHOLIC ARCHBISHOP

"Your Excellency"

A RABBI

"Rabbi _____"

A MEMBER OF THE PROTESTANT CLERGY

"Mr. _____," "Mrs. _____,"

"Ms. _____," or "Dr. _____"

Extremely formal moments at the dinner table

How to Use a Finger Bowl

If lobster or fresh fruit that must be peeled and eaten with your hands is served at a restaurant, a finger bowl may be placed on the table.

Either flowers or a slice of lemon will be floating in the bowl, so a gentleman will not make the mistake of drinking the finger bowl water.

A gentleman dips his fingers in the finger bowl to remove sticky juices or sauces. He dries his fingertips with his napkin. A server will remove the finger bowl as soon as it has served its purpose.

How to Eat Caviar

Caviar is most often served nowadays as an hors d'oeuvre, spread on wheat crackers or spooned on new potatoes. It may be served as a first course, presented on a small plate along with some crusts of bread and traditional accompaniments such as grated onion, grated egg, and capers.

A gentleman remembers that caviar is salty and a little goes a long way. He uses his napkin carefully, since black fish eggs can make an ugly stain on the front of his white shirt.

How to Eat an Artichoke

Usually an entire artichoke will be on your plate. Its leaves will point upward. A gentleman pulls each leaf off, dips it in the provided sauce, and scrapes it between his teeth to remove the tender flesh. Once all the leaves are gone, a hairy little island will remain in the middle of the artichoke. This is the "choke." A gentleman uses his knife and fork to slice it away, uncovering the delicious artichoke heart underneath. He cuts the heart into bite-size pieces and dips them in the sauce before eating them.

A finger bowl may be placed on the table so that a gentleman may clean his fingers.

How to Eat Snails

If a gentleman encounters snails— or *escargot* (pronounced "ess-car-go") at a dinner party, he will be provided with the necessary equipment for eating them. A special pair of tongs to grip the snail and a small fork for pulling the meat out of the shell will be provided. If no tongs are provided, the gentleman must use his fingers to hold the shell. He makes sure to get a good grip. Otherwise, the rounded shells may go sailing around the room.

The tiny shellfish fork is placed on the right side of the plate, outside the knife and spoon.

THE SCOOP OF SORBET

At some grand-scale banquets or formal restaurants, after the main course, a gentleman may be presented with a small scoop of citrus- or liqueur-flavored sorbet in a dish. This is not dessert. It is merely a break in the meal so that the tartness of the sorbet can clear away the heavy taste of the entrée. Sorbet is usually followed by a salad course.

A FINAL WORD

A gentleman never makes himself the center of attention.

His goal is to make life easier, not just for himself but for his friends, his acquaintances, and the world at large.

Because he is a gentleman, he does not see this as a burden. Instead, it is a challenge he faces eagerly every day.